This book belongs to

_____

_____

I am
VERY SPECIAL
to God!

Squishy, Squishy

A Book about My Five Senses

By Chérie B. Stihler

Illustrated by Heidi Rose

Pauline
BOOKS & MEDIA
Boston

Library of Congress Cataloging-in-Publication Data

Stihler, Chérie B.
   Squishy, squishy : a book about my five senses / by Cherie B. Stihler ; illustrated by
Heidi Rose.
      p. cm.
   ISBN 0-8198-7078-1 (pbk.)
   1. Senses and sensation—Religious aspects—Christianity—Juvenile literature. I.
Rose, Heidi. II. Title.
BT745.S74 2005
242'.62—dc22

2004016896

"P" and PAULINE are registered trademarks of the Daughters of St. Paul

Published by Pauline Books & Media, 50 Saint Pauls Avenue, Boston, MA 02130-3491.
Printed in Canada

www.pauline.org

Pauline Books & Media is the publishing house of the Daughters of St. Paul, an interna-
tional congregation of women religious serving the Church with the communications
media.

1 2 3 4 5 6 7 8 9   11 10 09 08 07 06 05

Squishy, squishy,
Cool and gooshy,
Mud squiggles between my toes.

6

I FEEL and SEE it. I HEAR it splash.
I SMELL the soil below.
But should I ever TASTE it?
Oh no, no! No, no, no!

MUD PIES
5¢ FRee!

Thank you, God,
for my FIVE SENSES!

Eggs and pancakes cooking,
bacon sizzling on the stove,
Gingerbread that's baking,
full of cinnamon and clove.

8

Giant pine trees in the park,
long green grass that's just been mowed,
Air so fresh after the rain,
pretty flowers by the road.

Thank you, God, for all of the wonderful things
I can SMELL!

9

A nice hot cup of cocoa
on a snowy winter day,
A twisty, minty candy cane
when I come in from play.

10

A salty bag of peanuts,
or a watermelon slice,
A tangy glass of lemonade,
with lots and lots of ice.

Thank you, God, for all of the wonderful things
I can TASTE!

Giggles, music, secrets,
and the little birds that sing,
Crash, KABOOM, rat-a-tat,
toot-toot and ring-a-ling.

12

My Mommy says, "Good morning,"
and my Daddy says, "Good night."
"We love you!" they both whisper
when they click on my night-light.

Thank you, God, for all of the wonderful things
I can HEAR!

13

Bumble bees and ladybugs,
a dancing dragonfly,
Sunshine on the flowers,
clouds and rainbows in the sky.

14

Cotton candy sunsets,
all orange, white, and pink,
Silvery stars at nighttime
that twinkle, shine, and blink.

Thank you, God, for all of the wonderful things
I can SEE!

Hard bricks on a fireplace,
smooth, cool windowpanes,
Lumpy, bumpy walnut shells,
chilly drops of rain.

16

Kitty, with her soft, warm fur,
purrs happily while she naps.
I'm snuggled up all cozy
for a story on a lap.

Thank you, God, for all of the
wonderful things I can TOUCH and feel!

17

Thank you, God, for my FIVE SENSES,
your special gifts to me!

Draw and color with markers pictures of more good things God gives you to SMELL.

Draw and color with markers pictures of more good things God gives you to TASTE.

Draw and color with markers pictures of more good things God gives you to HEAR.

Draw and color with markers pictures of more good things God gives you to SEE.

Draw and color with markers pictures of more good things God gives you to TOUCH and feel.

BOOKS & MEDIA

The Daughters of St. Paul operate book and media centers at the following addresses. Visit, call or write the one nearest you today, or find us on the World Wide Web, www.pauline.org

CALIFORNIA
3908 Sepulveda Blvd, Culver City, CA 90230	310-397-8676
5945 Balboa Avenue, San Diego, CA 92111	858-565-9181
46 Geary Street, San Francisco, CA 94108	415-781-5180

FLORIDA
145 S.W. 107th Avenue, Miami, FL 33174	305-559-6715

HAWAII
1143 Bishop Street, Honolulu, HI 96813	808-521-2731
Neighbor Islands call:	866-521-2731

ILLINOIS
172 North Michigan Avenue, Chicago, IL 60601	312-346-4228

LOUISIANA
4403 Veterans Memorial Blvd, Metairie, LA 70006	504-887-7631

MASSACHUSETTS
885 Providence Hwy, Dedham, MA 02026	781-326-5385

MISSOURI
9804 Watson Road, St. Louis, MO 63126	314-965-3512

NEW JERSEY
561 U.S. Route 1, Wick Plaza, Edison, NJ 08817	732-572-1200

NEW YORK
150 East 52nd Street, New York, NY 10022	212-754-1110
78 Fort Place, Staten Island, NY 10301	718-447-5071

PENNSYLVANIA
9171-A Roosevelt Blvd, Philadelphia, PA 19114	215-676-9494

SOUTH CAROLINA
243 King Street, Charleston, SC 29401	843-577-0175

TENNESSEE
4811 Poplar Avenue, Memphis, TN 38117	901-761-2987

TEXAS
114 Main Plaza, San Antonio, TX 78205	210-224-8101

VIRGINIA
1025 King Street, Alexandria, VA 22314	703-549-3806

CANADA
3022 Dufferin Street, Toronto, ON M6B 3T5	416-781-913

¡También somos su fuente para libros, videos y música en español!